VERSUS

ADIDAS vs PUMA
A LONG-RUNNING RIVALRY

KENNY ABDO

Fly!
An Imprint of Abdo Zoom
abdobooks.com

abdobooks.com

Published by Abdo Zoom, a division of ABDO, P.O. Box 398166, Minneapolis, Minnesota 55439. Copyright © 2023 by Abdo Consulting Group, Inc. International copyrights reserved in all countries. No part of this book may be reproduced in any form without written permission from the publisher. Fly!™ is a trademark and logo of Abdo Zoom.

Printed in the United States of America, North Mankato, Minnesota.
102022
012023

Photo Credits: Alamy, Getty Images, Shutterstock
Production Contributors: Kenny Abdo, Jennie Forsberg, Grace Hansen
Design Contributors: Candice Keimig, Neil Klinepier, Laura Graphenteen

Library of Congress Control Number: 2021950285

Publisher's Cataloging-in-Publication Data

Names: Abdo, Kenny, author.
Title: Adidas vs. Puma: a long-running rivalry / by Kenny Abdo.
Other title: a long-running rivalry
Description: Minneapolis, Minnesota : Abdo Zoom, 2023 | Series: Versus |
    Includes online resources and index.
Identifiers: ISBN 9781098228606 (lib. bdg.) | ISBN 9781098229443 (ebook) |
    ISBN 9781098229863 (Read-to-Me ebook)
Subjects: LCSH: Adidas AG--Juvenile literature. | PUMA AG Rudolf Dassler Sport
    -Juvenile literature. | Sport clothes industry--Juvenile literature. | Athletic
    shoes--Juvenile literature. | Competition--Economic aspects--Juvenile
    literature.
Classification: DDC 338.7--dc23

TABLE OF CONTENTS

Adidas vs. Puma 4

The Companies................. 8

Fight! 14

Legacy 18

Glossary 22

Online Resources 23

Index 24

ADIDAS vs PUMA

Puma and Adidas are two of the most recognizable shoe **brands** in the world. But the bad blood between the two companies goes beyond just business.

In Herzogenaurach, Germany, two brothers had the same dream. Their differences divided not only them, but the town that they lived in.

THE COMPANIES

Brothers Adolf and Rudolf Dassler wanted to create a shoe company.

Together in their mother's laundry room, they launched Geda Shoes in 1919.

Adolf designed and made the shoes. Rudolf sold them. Their business boomed after Geda became the official shoe of gold-medal-winning athletes in the 1936 **Olympics**.

After **WWII**, a rift formed between the brothers. To this day nobody knows what caused the dispute. Whatever happened, Geda was **shuttered** in 1948 and the men went their separate ways.

FIGHT!

In the same year, Rudolf created his own shoe company called Puma. Adolf opened Adidas in 1949. The name was a combination of his first and last name.

Puma and Adidas became very different shoe **brands** that **dominated** different areas of sports. Puma was designed for track and field. Adidas focused on soccer.

The brothers built competing factories on the opposite sides of the river in Herzogenaurach. The villagers chose a side, too! They looked down at each others shoes to decide who they could trust.

Rudolf passed away in 1974 in Germany. Adolf followed four years later. The brothers were buried in the same cemetery, but very far from each other. They had never **reconciled**.

LEGACY

Adidas is the second-most popular sports shoe in the world. The company is a major part of professional soccer.

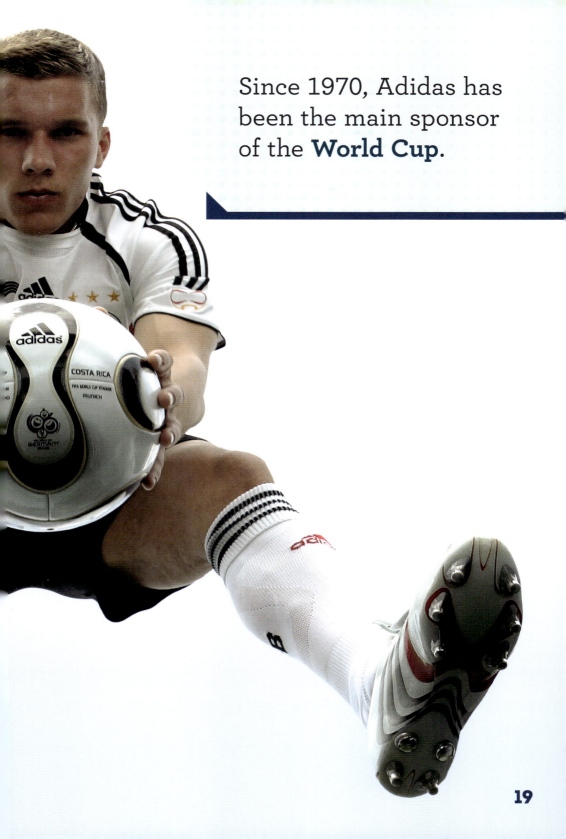

Since 1970, Adidas has been the main sponsor of the **World Cup**.

Puma has influenced many sports throughout the years. NBA player Kyle Kuzma signed with the **brand** in 2019. The **forward** filled the court with Puma's colorful and unique designs.

In 2009, Adidas and Puma made peace with a friendly soccer match. During United Nations World Peace Day, the companies did what their creators couldn't. The teams shook hands at the end.

GLOSSARY

brand – a name, design, or symbol that separates one product from another.

dominate – to have control over something.

forward – a position in basketball. They stay near the basket for rebounds and defense.

Olympic Games – the biggest sporting event in the world that is divided into summer and winter games.

reconcile – to make up or become friends again.

shutter – another way to say something has closed for good.

World Cup – an international soccer competition held every four years.

World War II (WWII) – from 1939 to 1945, fought in Europe, Asia, and Africa. Great Britain, France, the United States, the Soviet Union, and their allies were on one side. Germany, Italy, Japan, and their allies were on the other side.

ONLINE RESOURCES

To learn more about Adidas and Puma, please visit **abdobooklinks.com** or scan this QR code. These links are routinely monitored and updated to provide the most current information available.

INDEX

Dassler, Adolf 8, 10, 14, 17

Dassler, Rudolf 8, 10, 14, 17

Geda Shoes 9, 10, 12

Germany 6, 16

Kuzma, Kyle 20

National Basketball League (NBA) 20

Olympic Games 10

soccer 15, 18

United Nations World Peace Day 21

World Cup 19

World War II 12